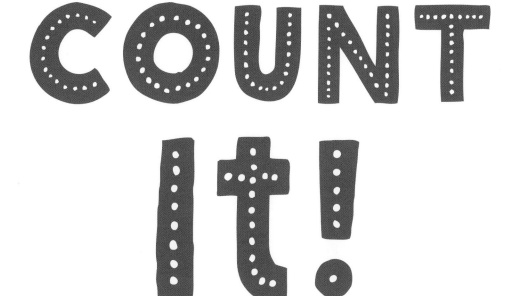

COUNT It!

RACHEL FIRST

Consulting Editor, Diane Craig, M.A./Reading Specialist

Sandcastle

An Imprint of Abdo Publishing
abdopublishing.com

abdopublishing.com

Published by Abdo Publishing, a division of ABDO, PO Box 398166, Minneapolis, Minnesota 55439. Copyright © 2016 by Abdo Consulting Group, Inc. International copyrights reserved in all countries. No part of this book may be reproduced in any form without written permission from the publisher. SandCastle™ is a trademark and logo of Abdo Publishing.

Printed in the United States of America, North Mankato, Minnesota
102015
012016

THIS BOOK CONTAINS
RECYCLED MATERIALS

Editor: Liz Salzmann
Content Developer: Nancy Tuminelly
Cover and Interior Design and Production: Mighty Media, Inc.
Photo Credits: Shutterstock

Library of Congress Cataloging-in-Publication Data

First, Rachel, author.
 Count it! : fun with counting & comparing / Rachel First ; consulting editor, Diane Craig, M.A./ reading specialist.
   pages cm. -- (Math beginnings)
 ISBN 978-1-62403-933-1
1. Counting--Juvenile literature. 2. Arithmetic--Juvenile literature. I. Title.
 QA113.F477 2016
 513.2--dc23
                    2015020584

SandCastle™ Level: Transitional

SandCastle™ books are created by a team of professional educators, reading specialists, and content developers around five essential components—phonemic awareness, phonics, vocabulary, text comprehension, and fluency—to assist young readers as they develop reading skills and strategies and increase their general knowledge. All books are written, reviewed, and leveled for guided reading, early reading intervention, and Accelerated Reader™ programs for use in shared, guided, and independent reading and writing activities to support a balanced approach to literacy instruction. The SandCastle™ series has four levels that correspond to early literacy development. The levels are provided to help teachers and parents select appropriate books for young readers.

EMERGING · BEGINNING · **TRANSITIONAL** · FLUENT

Contents

How Many?   4

Groups   10

Fewer or More?   14

Few or Many?   18

Practice   22

Glossary   24

HOW MANY?

It's fun to count things!

1   2   3

Counting tells us how many there are.

We use numbers to count
exact amounts.

Numbers go on **forever**.
How high can you count?

Claire
counts
beads.
She moves
each one.

ONE

TWO

She counts each one when she moves it.

THREE

She finds the exact amount.

GROUPS

Dylan makes rock piles.
How many piles does he make?
How many rocks are in each pile?

Lia and Zoe count **coins** at home.

They sort them. They make piles of **coins**. Each pile will have the same amount.

Try It!

Look around your house. What things can you sort and count?

FEWER or MORE?

Sometimes we compare amounts.

There are seven kids on Cal's soccer team. They have two soccer balls. There are fewer soccer balls than kids.

FEWER

MORE

You don't have to count to **compare**.
You can just look.

Ryan plays with toy animals.
He has more cows than dinosaurs.

FEW or MANY?

Sometimes *how much* is an **estimate.** Exact numbers are not used for estimates.

FEW

MANY

Anna has a few berries.
They fit on a spoon.

Luke has many berries.
They fill a jar!

Try It!

Look around. Make other **estimates**! What do you see a few of? What do you see many of?

PRACTICE

Find different small things. They could be blocks, pins, crayons, or anything! Sort them into piles by type. Don't count them yet!

Estimate and **compare**! Are there many or a few in each pile? Which pile has more? Which has fewer?

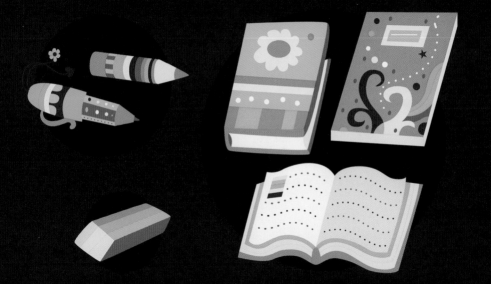

Then count the things. How many are there?

Glossary

COIN – a small, flat piece of metal used as money.

COMPARE – to decide how two or more things are different or the same.

ESTIMATE – an amount that is close to correct.

FOREVER – never-ending.